To Co[...]
with love from

Cynthia

DAILY

Stepping Stones

THE HELEN STEINER RICE FOUNDATION

Whatever the celebration, whatever the day, whatever the event, whatever the occasion, Helen Steiner Rice possessed the ability to express the appropriate feeling for that particular moment in time.

A happening became happier, a sentiment more sentimental, a memory more memorable because of her deep sensitivity to put into understandable language the emotion being experienced. Her positive attitude, her concern for others, and her love of God are identifiable threads woven into her life, her works . . . and even her death.

Prior to her passing, she established the HELEN STEINER RICE FOUNDATION, a nonprofit corporation whose purpose is to award grants to worthy charitable programs that aid the elderly, the needy, and the poor. In her lifetime, these were the individuals about whom Mrs. Rice was greatly concerned.

Royalties from the sale of this book will add to the financial capabilities of the HELEN STEINER RICE FOUNDATION, thus making possible additional grants. Each year this foundation presents grants, ranging from three thousand to fifteen thousand dollars each, to various, qualified, worthwhile, and charitable programs. Because of her foresight, her caring, and her deep convictions, Helen Steiner Rice continues to touch a countless number of lives. Thank you for your assistance in helping to keep Helen's dream alive.

Virginia J. Ruehlmann, Administrator

DAILY Stepping Stones

Helen Steiner Rice

Prayers by Virginia J. Ruehlmann

Fleming H. Revell Company
Tarrytown, New York

Unless otherwise indicated, the Scripture quotations in this book are taken from the Revised Standard Version of the Bible, Copyrighted © 1946, 1952, 1971, by the Division of Christian Education of the National Council of the Churches of Christ in the United States of America, and are used by permission. All rights reserved.

Scripture verses marked TLB are taken from The Living Bible, Copyright © 1971 by Tyndale House Publishers, Wheaton, Ill. Used by permission.

Scripture verses marked NAB are taken from the **New American Bible,** Copyright © 1970 by the Confraternity of Christian Doctrine, Washington, D.C. and are used by permission. All rights reserved.

Library of Congress Cataloging-in-Publication Data

Rice, Helen Steiner.
   Daily steppingstones / Helen Steiner Rice.
     p.   cm.
   ISBN 0-8007-1616-7
   1. Devotional calendars.   I. Title.
  BV4811.R52 1989
  242'.2—dc20   89-32210
                     CIP

Jacket and interior illustrations by Susanne DeMarco

Published by the Fleming H. Revell Company
Old Tappan, New Jersey 07675
Printed in the United States of America

Dedicated to my beloved family
of whom I am immensely proud.
I observe in their daily lives
reflections of the teachings
of Jesus.

Contents

Often we wish for a moment to reflect and respond to God's Word. Passages of Scripture, meaningful poems, and praise to God may ease stresses and strains and provide inspiration. Whenever we petition our Father for help or pray in thanksgiving we receive a special gift of peace from Him.

Whether the times and tides of your life are tumultuous or tranquil, take the opportunity to trust God and to thank Him. Create your own spiritual oasis, your own verdant pasture and reflect on His love for you. The poetry of Helen Steiner Rice will enable you to do this. Her ability to create bridges of consolation, encouragement, and inspiration has proven to be nothing less than remarkable.

Working on this devotional has been the source of many happy and delightful experiences. Researching appropriate Scriptures, reviewing the poetry of Helen Steiner Rice, and then supplying a suitable thought or meditation became a project of joy and a labor of love. Recollections, advice, and sayings told, taught, and prayed by my mother and grandmother often surfaced in my mind, prompting nostalgic memories of years long ago. My hope is that the reader will share the encouragement, the enjoyment, and the peace that this writer experienced in compiling these selections. May serenity and joy, comfort and inspiration be with you as you read this daily devotional.

VIRGINIA J. RUEHLMANN

Steppingstones

Think not that life has been unfair
And given you too much to bear . . .
For God has chosen you because
With all your weaknesses and flaws
He feels that you are worthy of
The greatness of His wondrous love.
Welcome every stumbling block
And every thorn and jagged rock,
For each one is a steppingstone
To a fuller life than we've ever known,
And in the radiance of God's smiles
We learn to soar above life's trials.
And as we grow in strength and grace
The clearer we can see God's face.

Blessings

Now faith is the assurance of things hoped for, the conviction of things not seen. For by it the men of old received divine approval. By faith we understand that the world was created by the word of God, so that what is seen was made out of things which do not appear.

Hebrews 11:1-3

My blessings are so many,
My troubles are so few,
How can I feel discouraged
When I know that I have You.
And I have the sweet assurance
That I'll never stand alone
If I but keep remembering
I am Yours and Yours alone. . .
So, in this world of trouble
With darkness all around,
Take my hand and lead me
Until I stand on higher ground.
For anything and everything
Can somehow be endured
If Your presence is beside me
And lovingly assured!

Father, keep my faith strong, my fervor constant. Although I cannot see You, I know You are always near, always at my side.

And this is what he has promised us, eternal life.

1 John 2:25

In this uncertain world of trouble
With its sorrow, sin, and strife
Man needs a haven for his heart
To endure the storms of life. . .
He keeps hoping for a promise
Of better, bigger things
With the power and the prestige
That fame and fortune bring. . .
And the world is rife with promises
That are fast and falsely spoken
For man in his deceptive way
Knows his promise can be broken. . .
But when God makes a promise
It remains forever true
For everything God promises
He unalterably will do. . .
And when you're disillusioned
And every hope is blighted
Recall the promises of God
And your faith will be relighted.

*Generous God, thank You for giving me everlasting life.
Keep the embers of faith aglow within me.*

Nevertheless the Lord your God would not hearken to Balaam; but the Lord your God turned the curse into a blessing for you, because the Lord your God loved you.

Deuteronomy 23:5

No one likes to be sick
   and yet we know
It takes sunshine and rain
   to make flowers grow. . .
And if we never were sick
   and never felt pain,
We'd be like a desert
   without any rain,
And who wants a life
   that is barren and dry
With never a cloud
   to darken the sky. . .
For continuous sun
   goes unrecognized
Like the blessings God sends
   which are often disguised,
For sometimes a sickness
   that seems so distressing
Is a time of renewal
   and a spiritual blessing.

Jesus, let my pathway of pain lead me to a garden of healing, a garden in which understanding and compassion are but two of the flowers. Plant me wherever You see fit. Cultivate me. Help me to grow, blossom, and bloom.

Bless the LORD, O my soul,
　and forget not all his benefits;
He pardons all your iniquities,
　he heals all your ills.
He redeems your life from destruction,
　he crowns you with kindness and compassion.

Psalms 103:2–4 NAB

When life has lost its luster
　　and it's filled with dull routine
When you long to run away from it
　　seeking pastures new and green
Remember, no one runs away from life
　　without finding when they do
You can't escape the thoughts you think
　　that are pressing down on you.
For though the scenery may be different
　　it's the same old heart and mind
And the same old restless longings
　　that you tried to leave behind.
So when your heart is heavy
　　and your day is dull with care
Instead of trying to escape
　　why not withdraw in prayer
For in prayer there is renewal
　　of the spirit, mind, and heart
For everything is lifted up
　　in which God has a part.

Father, I come to You today asking if You will rearrange my thoughts and renew me in spirit, mind, and heart. In prayer I offer my heart to You.

Blessed is the man whom thou dost chasten, O Lord, and whom thou dost teach out of thy law to give him respite from days of trouble. . . . For the Lord will not forsake his people. . . .

Psalms 94:12–14

> While it's very difficult
> for mankind to understand
> God's intentions and His purpose
> and the workings of His hand,
> If we observe the miracles
> that happen every day,
> We cannot help but be convinced
> that in His wondrous way
> God makes what seemed unbearable
> and painful and distressing
> Easily acceptable
> when we view it as a blessing.

In every trouble or problem, there is a blessing. It takes patience and perseverence to see it. Improve my outlook, Lord, so that I can see clearly the blessing You have sent my way.

"Ask and it will be given you; seek, and you will find; knock, and it will be opened to you. . . . If you then, who are evil, know how to give good gifts to your children, how much more wil your Father who is in heaven give good things to those who ask him!"

Matthew 7:7, 11

Each day there are showers of blessings
Sent from the Father above,
For God is a great, lavish giver
And there is no end to His love—
His grace is more than sufficient,
His mercy is boundless and deep,
And His infinite blessings are countless
And all this we're given to keep
If we but seek God and find Him
And ask for a bounteous measure
Of this wholly immeasurable offering
From God's inexhaustible treasure—
For no matter how big man's dreams are,
God's blessings are infinitely more,
For always God's giving is greater
Than what man is asking for.

Father, Your blessings are all around me. Have I thanked You for Your generosity, Your mercy, and Your love?

Praise the Lord! Praise, O servants of the Lord, praise the name of the Lord! Blessed be the name of the Lord from this time forth and for evermore! From the rising of the sun to its setting the name of the Lord is to be praised!

Psalms 113:1–3

The good, green earth beneath our feet,
The air we breathe, the food we eat,
Some work to do, a goal to win,
A hidden longing deep within
That spurs us on to bigger things
And helps us meet what each day brings,
All these things and many more
Are things we should be thankful for. . .
And most of all our thankful prayers
Should rise to God because He cares!

Thank You, Father, for the many blessings—visible and invisible—that You have bestowed upon me.

New Life

The Lord is gracious and merciful, slow to anger and abounding in steadfast love. The Lord is good to all, and his compassion is over all that he has made.

Psalms 145:8, 9

"The earth is the Lord's
    and the fulness thereof"—
It speaks of His greatness
    and it sings of His love.
Through all of creation
    with symphonic splendor
God speaks with a voice
    that is gentle and tender.
And the birds in the trees
    and the flowers of spring
All join in proclaiming
    this heavenly King.

Father God, when I think of the wonders which You have created and the glory of Your power, I am overwhelmed with love and admiration.

A voice says, "Cry!" And I said, "What shall I cry?"
All flesh is grass, and all its beauty is like the flower
of the field. The grass withers, the flower fades,
when the breath of the Lord blows upon it; surely the
people is grass. The grass withers, the flower fades;
but the word of our God will stand for ever.

Isaiah 40:6–8

All nature heeds the call of spring
As God awakens everything,
And all that seemed
so dead and still
Experiences a sudden thrill

As springtime lays a magic hand
Across God's vast and fertile land—
Oh, how can anyone
stand by
And watch a sapphire springtime sky,

Or see a fragile flower break through
What just a day ago or two
Seemed barren ground
still hard with frost,
But in God's world no life is lost,

And flowers sleep beneath the ground
But when they hear spring's waking sound
They push themselves
through layers of clay
To reach the sunlight of God's Day.

*Jesus, help me to realize that I am a seed planted in my
Master's garden but I can grow and blossom and become a
flower worthy to be picked and placed in His bouquet.*

We were buried therefore with him by baptism into death, so that as Christ was raised from the dead by the glory of the Father, we too might walk in newness of life.

Romans 6:4

And in the resurrection
That takes place in nature's sod
Let us understand more fully
The risen son of God.
And let us see the beauty
And the glory and the grace
That surrounds us in the springtime
as the smiling of God's face.
And through a happy springtime
and a summer filled with love
May we walk into the autumn
With our thoughts on God above:
The God who sends the winter
and wraps the earth in death
Will always send the springtime
with an awakening breath
To every flower and leaflet
And to every shrub and tree
And that same God will also send
new life to you and me.

Whatever the season, whatever the time of year, let me make time to praise You Lord for the new life that continues to appear.

". . . As the branch cannot bear fruit by itself, unless it abides in the vine, neither can you, unless you abide in me. I am the vine, you are the branches. He who abides in me, and I in him, he it is that bears much fruit, for apart from me you can do nothing."

John 15:4, 5

Apple blossoms bursting wide
   now beautify the tree
And make a springtime picture
   that is beautiful to see. . .
Oh, fragrant lovely blossoms,
   you'll make a bright bouquet
If I but break your branches
   from the apple tree today. . .
But if I break your branches
   and make your beauty mine,
You'll bear no fruit in season
   when severed from the vine.

One True Vine, this branch is weakening. Nourish me so that I can bear fruit for Your harvest.

Man's days are like those of grass;
   like a flower of the field he blooms;
The wind sweeps over him and he is gone
   and his place knows him no more.
But the kindness of the LORD is from eternity
   to eternity toward those who fear him. . . .

Psalms 103:15–17 NAB

Spring is God's way
of speaking to men
And saying, "Through Me
you will live again."
For death is a season
that man must pass through
And, just like the flowers,
God awakens him, too.

Loving Father, if I did not go to sleep tonight I would not be refreshed for tomorrow. If the flowers did not rest in the winter they would not bloom next spring. Help me to remember that You who awaken the flowers will also awaken and welcome me at the appointed time.

And let us not grow weary in well-doing, for in due season we shall reap, if we do not lose heart.

Galatians 6:9

God grant this little springtime prayer
And make our hearts grown cold with care
Once more aware of the waking earth
Now pregnant with life and bursting with birth—
For how can man feel any fear or doubt
When on every side all around and about
The March winds blow across man's face
And whisper of God's power and grace—
Oh, give us faith to believe again
That peace on earth, good will to men
Will follow this winter of man's mind
And awaken his heart and make him kind—
And just as great nature sends the spring
To give new birth to each sleeping thing,
God grant rebirth to man's slumbering soul
And help him forsake his selfish goal.

. . . Refresh, renew, restore me, Dear Creator, and let me respond to Your requests.

Let the field exult, and everything in it! Then shall all the trees of the wood sing for joy.

Psalms 96:12

The sleeping earth awakens,
    The robins start to sing,
The flowers open wide their eyes
    To tell us it is spring,
The bleakness of the winter
    Is melted by the sun,
The tree that looked so stark and dead
    Becomes a living one. . .
These miracles of nature
    Wrought with divine perfection,
Are the blessed reassurance
    Of our Savior's Resurrection.

Miracle of miracles is that my Savior has risen and that He lives. Divine Miracle Worker, do a miraculous thing in my life today.

You have been born anew, not of perishable seed but of imperishable, through the living and abiding word of God; for "All flesh is like grass and all its glory like the flower of grass. The grass withers, and the flower falls, but the word of the Lord abides for ever."

1 Peter 1:23–25

The waking earth in springtime
Reminds us it is true
That nothing really ever dies
That will not rise anew. . .
So trust God's all-wise wisdom
And doubt the Father never,
For in His Heavenly Kingdom
You'll live with Him forever.

What a glorious and exciting sight to observe the earth awakening in springtime. What an even more exciting day when I am born anew.

Make a joyful noise to the Lord, all the lands! Serve the Lord with gladness! Come into his presence with singing!

Psalms 100:1, 2

In each waking flower and each singing bird,
The promise of new life is witnessed and heard.
Spring is God's way of speaking to men
And renewing the promise of Easter again
For death is a season that we must pass through,
And, just like the flowers, God will waken us too. . .
So why should we grieve when our loved ones die,
For we'll meet them again in a cloudless sky.

Father, let me place my life in its entirety in Your hands. Renew me as You renew the earth with Your loving touch.

When I look at thy heavens, the work of thy fingers, the moon and the stars which thou hast established; what is man that thou art mindful of him, and the son of man that thou dost care for him?

Psalms 8:3, 4

In everything both great and small
We see the hand of God in all,
And in the miracles of spring
When everywhere in everything
His handiwork is all around
And every lovely sight and sound
Proclaims the God of earth and sky
I ask myself "Just who am I"
That God should send His only Son
That my salvation would be won
For Jesus suffered, bled, and died
That sinners might be sanctified,
And to grant God's children such as I
Eternal life in Heaven on High.

Jesus, You gave up everything on this earth, even Your life, so that I might have something. You opened the door to eternal life. May I never disappoint You.

"I am the good shepherd. The good shepherd lays down his life for the sheep."

John 10:11

If we but had the eyes to see
God's face in every cloud,
If we but had the ears to hear
His voice above the crowd
If we could feel His gentle touch
In every springtime breeze
And find a haven in His arms
'Neath sheltering, leafy trees. . .
If we could just lift up our hearts
Like flowers to the sun
And trust His loving *promise*
And pray, *"Thy will be done,"*
We'd find the peace we're seeking,
The kind no man can give,
The peace that comes from knowing
He died so we might live!

Jesus, my loving Savior, You willingly died so that I might live. Let me willingly live in a way that is pleasing to You. Do not forsake me as I try.

29

Friendship

. . . and they shall be radiant over the goodness of the Lord, over the grain, the wine, and the oil, and over the young of the flock and the herd; their life shall be like a watered garden, and they shall languish no more.

Jeremiah 31:12

> Life is a garden,
>> Good friends are the flowers,
> And times spent together,
>> Life's happiest hours;
> And friendship, like flowers,
>> Blooms ever more fair
> When carefully tended
>> By dear friends who care;
> And life's lovely garden
>> Would be sweeter by far
> If all who passed through it
>> Were as nice as you are.

Caretaker of my Garden of Life, bless me with Your presence. Walk in my garden with me. Share some precious moments with me, my most valued Friend.

"Then the King will say to those at his right hand, 'Come, O blessed of my Father, inherit the kingdom prepared for you from the foundation of the world; for I was hungry and you gave me food, I was thirsty and you gave me drink, I was a stranger and you welcomed me.' "

Matthew 25:34–36

God knows no strangers,
 He loves us all,
The poor, the rich,
 The great, the small. . .
He is a friend
 Who is always there
To share our troubles
 And lessen our care. . .
No one is a stranger
 In God's sight,
For God is love
 And in His light
May we, too, try
 In our small way
To make new friends
 From day to day. . .
So pass no stranger
 With an unseeing eye,
For God may be sending
 A new friend by.

Loving and kind Jesus, I pray that You make me a more loving and considerate individual. Today, permit me to reach out to others with an open mind and an open heart.

Every one helps his neighbor, and says to his brother, "Take courage!"

Isaiah 41:6

It's not fortune
or fame
or worldwide acclaim
That makes for
true greatness,
you'll find—
It's the wonderful art
of teaching the heart
to always
be thoughtful
and kind!

Father, we all need some encouragement in our lives. Teach me how to be kind and thoughtful and how to elevate someone's self-esteem. Gentleness, kindness, and encouragement are indicators of a special strength. Instill that strength within me.

Your own friend and your father's friend
forsake not. . . .

Proverbs 27:10 NAB

So many things in the line of duty
Drain us of effort and leave us no beauty
And the dust of the soul grows thick and unswept
And spirit is drenched in tears unwept
But just as we fall beside the road
Discouraged with life and bowed down with our load
We lift our eyes, and what seemed a dead end
Is the street of dreams where we meet a friend.

Dear Father, when I see a friend, I see You.

Whoever confesses that Jesus is the Son of God, God abides in him, and he in God. So we know and believe the love God has for us. God is love, and he who abides in love abides in God, and God abides in him.

1 John 4:15, 16

Love is like magic and it always will be,
For love still remains life's sweet mystery!

Love works in ways that are wondrous and strange
And there's nothing in life that love cannot change!

Love can transform the most commonplace
Into beauty and splendor and sweetness and grace!

Love is unselfish, understanding, and kind,
For it sees with its heart and not with its mind!

Love gives and forgives, there is nothing too much
For love to heal with its magic touch!

Love is the language that every heart speaks,
For love is the one thing that every heart seeks!

Loving Jesus, help me to express my love for my fellowman even when my fellowman does not behave in a loving way to me.

Love one another with brotherly affection; outdo one another in showing honor. Never flag in zeal, be aglow with the Spirit, serve the Lord.

Romans 12:10, 11

I've never seen God
but I know how I feel,
It's people like you
who make Him so real. . .
It seems that I pass Him
so often each day
In the faces of people I meet on my way. . .
He's the stars in the heaven,
a smile on some face,
A leaf on a tree or a rose in a vase. . .
He's winter and autumn
and summer and spring. . .
In short, God is every
real, wonderful thing. . .
I wish I might meet Him
much more than I do,
I would if there were
More people like you.

Jesus, may I always realize that Your love is reflected in others. May I live my life so that others can see Your love reflected in me.

Let brotherly love continue. Do not neglect to show hospitality to strangers, for thereby some have entertained angels unawares.

Hebrews 13:1, 2

On life's busy thoroughfares
We meet with angels unawares—
So, Father, make us kind and wise
So we may always recognize
The blessings that are ours to take,
The friendships that are ours to make
If we but open our heart's door wide
To let the sunshine of love inside—
For God is not in far distant places
But in loving hearts and friendly faces.

Father, to have friends of my own, remind me that I must first reach out and be a friend.

"He who withholds kindness from a friend forsakes the fear of the Almighty."

Job 6:14

It's not the things that can be bought
    that are life's richest treasure,
It's just the little heart gifts
    that money cannot measure. . .
A cheerful smile, a friendly word,
    a sympathetic nod
Are priceless little treasures
    from the storehouse of our God. . .
They are the things that can't be bought
    with silver or with gold,
For thoughtfulness and kindness
    and love are never sold. . .
They are the priceless things in life
    for which no one can pay,
And the giver finds rich recompense
    in giving them away.

Forgive my insensitive nature, my selfish, materialistic outlook! Every real and lasting treasure is found only through You, God.

"A new commandment I give to you, that you love one another; even as I have loved you, that you also love one another."

John 13:34

If people like me
    didn't know people like you
Life would lose its meaning
    and its richness too.
For the friends that we make
    are life's gift of love
and I think friends are
    sent right from heaven above.
And thinking of you
    somehow makes me feel. . .
That God is love
    and He's very real

There is no Friend like You, Jesus, and what a true Friend You are!

Trials &
Tribulations

Humble yourselves therefore under the mighty hand of God, that in due time he may exalt you. Cast all your anxieties on him, for he cares about you.

1 Peter 5:6, 7

Let us go quietly to God
        when troubles come to us,
Let us never stop to whimper
        or complain and fret and fuss,
Let us hide our thorns in roses
        and our sighs in golden song
And our crosses in a crown of smiles
        whenever things go wrong. . .
For no one can really help us
        as our troubles we bemoan,
For comfort, help, and inner peace
        must come from God alone. . .
So do not tell your neighbor,
        your companion or your friend
In the hope that they can help you
        bring your troubles to an end. . .
For they, too, have their problems,
        they are burdened just like you,
So take your cross to Jesus
        and He will see you through.

Talk to me, Jesus, and heal my heartsick loneliness. Why should I be downcast when I have You for my Friend?

Justice will bring about peace;
   right will produce calm and security.
My people will live in peaceful country,
   in secure dwellings and quiet resting places.

Isaiah 32:17–19 NAB

Sometimes the road of life seems long
   as we travel through the years
And, with a heart that's broken
   and eyes brimful of tears,
We falter in our weariness
   and sink beside the way,
But God leans down and whispers,
   "Child, there'll be another day"—
And the road will grow much smoother
   and much easier to face,
So do not be disheartened—
   this is just a resting place.

Creator, send a message of hope and love to me today. Help me to remember that the sun is in the heavens each and every day—even when it's raining! Permit me to see the rainbows in my own backyard.

I will make my people and their homes around my hill a blessing. And there shall be showers, showers of blessing, for I will not shut off the rains but send them in their seasons.

Ezekiel 34:26 TLB

God, give us wider vision
      to see and understand
That both the sun and showers
      are gifts from Thy great hand,
And teach us that it takes the showers
      to make the flowers grow
And only in the storms of life
      when the winds of trouble blow
Can man, too, reach maturity
      and grow in faith and grace
And gain the strength and courage
      to enable him to face
Sunny days as well as rain,
      high peaks as well as low,
Knowing that the "April Showers
      will make the May Flowers Grow"—
And then at last may we accept
      "the Sunshine and the Showers,"
Confident it takes them both
      to make Salvation ours!

Cultivate within me all those qualities You want to see there, God. Let me grow in understanding and may kindness flourish within me.

Keep your life free from love of money, and be content with what you have; for he has said, "I will never fail you nor forsake you."

Hebrews 13:5

In the deep, dark hours of my distress
My unworthy life seems a miserable mess—
Handicapped, limited, with my strength decreasing
The demands on my time keep forever increasing
And I pray for the flair and the force of youth
So I can keep spreading God's light and His truth. . .
So let me say no to all flattery and praise
And quietly spend the rest of my days
Far from the greed of man
Who has so distorted God's simple life plan. . .
And let me be great in the eyes of the Lord
For that is the richest, most priceless reward.

Holy Spirit, each one of us here on earth needs admiration, affection, appreciation, and approval. I shall endeavor to be a source of these qualities. When tossing a pebble into a lake, it's impossible to predict the flow and the magnitude of the ripples. So, too, I can only imagine how far-reaching my efforts will be.

Jesus said to all: "Whoever wishes to be my follower must deny his very self, take up his cross each day, and follow in my steps."

Luke 9:23 NAB

We all have those days
    that are dismal and dreary
And we feel sort of blue
    and lonely and weary,
But we have to admit
    that life is worth living
And God gives us reasons
    for daily thanksgiving. . .
For each trial we suffer
    and every shed tear
Just gives us new strength
    to persevere
As we climb the steep hills
    along life's way
That lead us at last
    to that wonderful day
Where the cross we have carried
    becomes a crown
And at last we can lay
    Our burden down!

Lord, carrying my cross conditions and strengthens my muscles. It will enable me to raise the crown to my head on that wonderful day that is yet to come.

45

I have fought the good fight, I have finished the race,
I have kept the faith. Henceforth there is laid up for
me the crown of righteousness. . . .

2 Timothy 4:7, 8

Oh, spare me all trouble and save me from sorrow
May each happy day bring a brighter tomorrow.
May I never know pain or taste bitter woe
Sadness and suffering I care not to know.
But if I should meet Him sometime, face to face
Will I feel oddly strange and a bit out of place
When I look at the marks where the nails went in
As He hung on the cross to save us from sin?
Will He think me unworthy to be one of His own
And too weak and untried to sit at His throne?
Will I forfeit my right to a crown set with stars
Because I can show Him no battle scars?
Will the one who suffered and wept with pain
Be the one He will welcome to share His domain?
Will the trials of life make a crown of stars
Unfit to be worn by one without scars?

*Let me accept uncomplainingly the cross that You have
planned for me. Help me realize that everyone has or had a
cross to bear . . . even Your Son, Jesus.*

46

Later, in one of his talks, Jesus said to the people, "I am the Light of the world. So if you follow me, you won't be stumbling through the darkness, for living light will flood your path."

John 8:12 TLB

If I can endure for this minute
Whatever is happening to me,
No matter how heavy my heart is
Or how dark the moment may be—
If I can remain calm and quiet
With all my world crashing about me,
Secure in the knowledge God loves me
When everyone else seems to doubt me—
If I can but keep on believing
What I know in my heart to be true,
That darkness will fade with the morning
And that this will pass away, too—
Then nothing in life can defeat me
For as long as this knowledge remains
I can suffer whatever is happening
For I know God will break all the chains
That are binding me tight in the darkness
And trying to fill me with fear—
For there is no night without dawning
And I know that my morning is near.

Light of the world, lead me out of darkness. Develop within me the confidence that a new day will dawn and with it new hope.

Into your hands I commend my spirit;
you will redeem me, O LORD, O faithful God.

Psalms 31:6 NAB

I am perplexed and often vexed
And sometimes I cry and sadly sigh,
But do not think, dear Father above,
I question You or Your unchanging love—
It's just sometimes when I reach out
You seem to be nowhere about. . .
And while I am sure that You love me still
And I know in my heart that You always will,
Somehow I feel You are out of my reach,
And though I get down on my knees and beseech,
I cannot bring You closer to me
And I feel adrift on life's raging sea. . .
And though I cannot find Your hand
To lead me on to the Promised Land,
I still believe with all my being
Your hand is there beyond my seeing!

Father, help me to place my hand and my life into Your hands.

The Lord bless you and keep you: The Lord make his face to shine upon you, and be gracious to you: The Lord lift up his countenance upon you, and give you peace.

Numbers 6:24–26

God speaks to us in many ways,
Altering our lives, our plans, and days,
And His blessings come in many guises
That He alone in love devises,
And sorrow that we dread so much
Can bring a very healing touch—
For when we fail to heed His voice,
We leave the Lord no other choice
Except to use a firm, stern hand
To make us know He's in command—
For on the wings of loss and pain
The peace we often sought in vain
Will come to us with sweet surprise
For God is merciful and wise—
And through dark hours of tribulation
God gives us time for meditation,
And nothing can be counted loss
That teaches us to bear our cross!

Dear God, speak to me, alter my life, teach me to bear my cross. Heal me and love me.

None of us lives to himself, and none of us dies to himself. If we live, we live to the Lord, and if we die, we die to the Lord; so then, whether we live or whether we die, we are the Lord's.

Romans 14:7, 8

Why am I impatient
and continually vexed,
And often bewildered,
disturbed, and perplexed?
I'm working so tensely
in my self-centered way,
I've no time to listen
for what God has to say.
And hard as I work,
at the end of the day
I know in my heart
I did not pay my way.
But God in His mercy
looks down on us all
And though what we've done
is so pitifully small
He makes us feel welcome
to kneel down and pray
For the chance to do better
as we start a new day!

As I start a new day, let me resolve to remove harsh words from my speech. Once spoken, words are unretrievable. Teach me, God, to always speak with compassion and understanding.

Share each other's troubles and problems, and so obey our Lord's command. . . . Let everyone be sure that he is doing his very best, for then he will have the personal satisfaction of work well done, and won't need to compare himself with someone else. Each of us must bear some faults and burdens of his own. For none of us is perfect!

Galatians 6:2, 4, 5 TLB

As we travel down life's busy road
Complaining of our heavy load,
We often think God's been unfair
And given us more than our share
Of little daily irritations
And disappointing tribulations. . .
We're discontented with our lot
And all the bad breaks that we got,
We count our losses, not our gain,
And remember only tears and pain. . .
And wrapped up in our own despair
We have no time to see or share
Another's load that far outweighs
Our little problems and dismays. . .
But if we'd but forget our care
And stop in sympathy to share
The burden that our brother carried,
Our mind and heart would be less harried
And we would feel our load was small,
In fact, we carried no load at all.

My burdens, Your burdens, our burdens! Burdens are with us every day. Let me share someone else's burden today, Lord, for then I shall be helping You.

Prayer

There is no fear in love, but perfect love casts out fear. For fear has to do with punishment, and he who fears is not perfected in love. We love, because he first loved us.

1 John 4:18, 19

On the wings of prayer
　　our burdens take flight
And our load of care
　　becomes bearably light,
And our heavy hearts
　　are lifted above
To be healed by the balm
　　of God's wonderful love,
And the tears in our eyes
　　are dried by the hands
Of a loving Father
　　who understands
All of our problems,
　　our fears and despair,
When we take them to Him
　　on the wings of prayer.

Jesus, shape my life and change my offensive ways. Teach me Your gentle manner of handling obstacles. Assist me in being a better person and not a bitter one.

And this is the confidence which we have in him, that
if we ask anything according to his will he hears us.

1 John 5:14

You're worried and troubled
 about everything,
Wondering and fearing
 what tomorrow will bring—
You long to tell someone
 for you feel so alone,
But your friends are all burdened
 with cares of their own—
There is only one place
 and only one Friend
Who is never too busy
 and you can always depend
That He will be waiting
 with arms open wide
To hear all your troubles
 that you came to confide—
For the heavenly Father
 will always be there
When you seek Him and find Him
 at the altar of prayer.

*Lord, You are the one Friend who is never too busy to take
time to listen to my problems. When I have made a foolish
error, You are the one Friend who still believes in me and
assures me that I have hope for improvement.*

. . . The doors were shut, but Jesus came and stood among them, and said, "Peace be with you."

John 20:26

Beyond that which words can interpret
or theology can explain
the soul feels a shower of refreshment
that falls like the gentle rain
on hearts that are parched with problems
and are searching to find the way
to somehow attract God's attention
through well-chosen words as they pray,
not knowing that God in His wisdom
can sense all man's worry and woe
for there is nothing man can conceal
that God does not already know. . .
So kneel in prayer in His presence
and you'll find no need to speak
for softly in silent communion
God grants you the peace that you seek.

Loving God, You washed the face of the earth last night with Your pure and much needed rain. Today, everything smells so clean, so fresh. Will You please refresh me also? Give me the same kind of peaceful feeling that I experience after a thunderstorm.

And they heard the sound of the Lord God walking
in the garden in the cool of the day. . . .

Genesis 3:8

My garden beautifies my yard
    and adds fragrance to the air. . .
But it is also my cathedral
    and my quiet place of prayer. . .
So little do we realize
    that the glory and the power
of He who made the universe
    lies hidden in a flower.

*Each time I gaze upon a flower, I see hidden there the
miracle, the marvel, and the power of You, our loving
Creator.*

Reflect on the precepts of the Lord,
  let his commandments be your constant meditation;
Then he will enlighten your mind,
  and the wisdom you desire he will grant.

Sirach 6:37 NAB

So we may know God better
And feel His quiet power,
Let us daily keep in silence
A meditation hour—
For to understand God's greatness
And to use His gifts each day
The soul must learn to meet Him
In a meditative way,
For nature's greatest forces
Are found in quiet things
Like softly falling snowflakes
Drifting down on angels' wings,
Or petals dropping soundlessly
From a lovely full-blown rose,
So God comes closest to us
When our souls are in repose.

Be still my soul, and quietly, silently, listen for a message from God.

"Therefore I tell you, whatever you ask in prayer, believe that you receive it, and you will."

Mark 11:24

We all have cares and problems
    we cannot solve alone
But if we go to God in prayer
    we are never on our own. . .
And if we try to stand alone
    we are weak and we will fall,
For God is always greatest
    when we're helpless, lost, and small.
And no day is unmeetable
    if on rising our first thought
Is to thank God for the blessings
    that His loving care has brought. . .
For there can be no failures
    or hopeless, unsaved sinners
If we enlist the help of God
    who makes all losers winners.

God, You are the greatest Problem Solver of all. I pray that You guide me in solving the problems facing me. May I realize that one is not a loser for failing in an attempt to accomplish something but rather, failure lies in never to have tried at all.

Trust in the Lord with all your heart, and do not rely on your own insight. In all your ways acknowledge him, and he will make straight your paths.

Proverbs 3:5, 6

Dear God, I keep praying for the things I desire,
   You tell me I'm selfish and "playing with fire"
It is hard to believe I am selfish and vain,
   My desires seem so real and my needs seem so
   sane,
And yet You are wiser and Your vision is wide
   And You look down on me and You see deep
   inside,
Oh, teach me, dear God, to not rush ahead
But to pray for Your guidance and to trust You
   instead,
For You know what I need and that I'm only a slave
To the things that I want and desire and crave—
Oh, God, in your mercy look down on me now
And see in my heart that I love You somehow—
Although in my rashness, impatience, and greed
I pray for the things that I want and don't need—
And instead of a crown please send me a cross
And teach me to know that all gain is but loss,
And show me the way to joy without end,
With You as my Father, Redeemer, and Friend.

Jesus, stay by my side for with You near to me all temptations lose their appeal and power.

"From the fig tree learn its lesson: as soon as its branch becomes tender and puts forth its leaves, you know that summer is near. So also when you see these things taking place, you know that he is near, at the very gates."

Mark 13:28, 29

I come to meet You God . . . and as I linger here
    I seem to feel You very near.
A rustling leaf . . . a rolling slope. . .
    speaks to my heart of endless hope.
The sun just rising in the sky,
    the waking birdlings as they fly,
The grass all wet with morning dew
    are telling me I've just met You!
And gently thus the day is born
    and night gives way to breaking morn
And once again I've met You, God
    and worshiped on Your holy sod
For who can see the dawn break through
    Without a glimpse of heaven and You?
For who but God could make the day
    and softly put the night away.

Let me welcome the morning and bid the evening adieu with You, Heavenly Creator, as my Companion.

But I will call upon God,
and the LORD will save me.
In the evening, and at dawn, and at noon,
I will grieve and moan,
and he will hear my voice.

Psalms 55:17, 18 NAB

Were you too busy this morning
to quietly stop and pray
Did you hurry and drink your coffee
then frantically rush away?
Consoling yourself by saying,
"God will always be there
Waiting to hear my petitions
ready to answer each prayer"
It's true the great generous Savior
forgives our transgressions each day
And patiently waits for lost sheep
who constantly seem to stray—
But moments of prayer once omitted
in the busy rush of the day
Can never again be recaptured
for they silently slip away.
So seek the Lord in the morning
and never forget Him at night
For prayer is an unfailing blessing
that makes every burden seem light.

Dear God, I hunger for You in my daily life. Do not forsake me but visit with me morning, noon, and night.

Love

"I am the true vine, and my Father is the vinedresser. Every branch of mine that bears no fruit, he takes away, and every branch that does bear fruit he prunes, that it may bear more fruit. You are already made clean by the word which I have spoken to you. Abide in me, and I in you. . . ."

John 15:1–5

When we cut ourselves away
    from guidance that's divine,
Our lives will be as fruitless
    as the branch without the vine
For as the flowering branches
    depend upon the tree
To nourish and fulfill them
    till they reach futurity,
We too must be dependent
    on our Father up above
For we are but the branches
    and He's the Tree of Love.

Tree of Love, let this branch flower and grow. Abide in me. Prune me when necessary, but please do not let me be cut away from You.

For God so loved the world that he gave his only Son, that whoever believes in him should not perish but have eternal life.

John 3:16

What is love?
No words can define it,
It's something so great
Only God could design it. . .
Wonder of wonders;
Beyond man's conception,
And only in God
Can love find true perfection,
For love means much more
Than small words can express,
For what man calls love
Is so very much less
Than the beauty and depth
And the true richness of
God's gift to mankind—
His compassionate love.

True love has been epitomized by You, Jesus. The truth of true love lies in the observation that one should be more concerned with being loving *than with being* loved.

Every man shall give as he is able, according to the blessing of the Lord your God which he has given you.

Deuteronomy 16:17

Time is not measured
by the years that you live
But by the deeds that you do
and the joy that you give—
And each day as it comes
brings a chance to each one
To love to the fullest,
leaving nothing undone
That would brighten the life
or lighten the load
Of some weary traveler
lost on life's road—
So what does it matter
how long we may live
If as long as we live
we unselfishly give.

Father, I have memorized the Golden Rule of "Do unto others as you would have them do unto you." Help me to put it into practice in my life and to really live by it.

"This is the covenant that I will make with them after those days, says the Lord: I will put my laws on their hearts, and write them on their minds," then he adds, "I will remember their sins and their misdeeds no more." Where there is forgiveness of these, there is no longer any offering for sin.

Hebrews 10:16–18

Oh, God, who made the summer
    and warmed the earth with beauty,
Warm our hearts with gratitude
    and devotion to our duty,
For in this age of violence,
    rebellion, and defiance
We've forgotten the true meaning
    of dependable reliance—
Our standards have been lowered
    and we resist all discipline,
And our vision has been narrowed
    and blinded to all sin—
Oh, put the summer brightness
    in our closed, unseeing eyes
So in the careworn faces
    that we pass we'll recognize
The heartbreak and the loneliness,
    the trouble and despair
That a word of understanding
    would make easier to bear—
Oh, God, look down on our cold hearts
    and warm them with Your love,
And grant us Your forgiveness
    which we're so unworthy of.

God, warm my heart with Your love so that I can reach out to others with warmth and tenderness.

Love is patient; love is kind. Love is not jealous, it does not put on airs, it is not snobbish. Love is never rude, it is not self-seeking, it is not prone to anger; neither does it brood over injuries. Love does not rejoice in what is wrong but rejoices with the truth. There is no limit to love's forbearance, to its trust, its hope, its power to endure.

1 Corinthians 13:4–7 NAB

Love is enduring
And patient and kind,
It judges all things
With the heart not the mind,
And love can transform
The most commonplace
Into beauty and splendor
And sweetness and grace.
For love is unselfish,
Giving more than it takes,
And no matter what happens
Love never forsakes,
It's faithful and trusting
And always believing,
Guileless and honest
And never deceiving.
Yes, love is beyond
What man can define,
For love is immortal
And God's gift is divine!

Dear God, You love us all. . . . No matter who or what we are. Grant that I may possess a portion of Your love and let me show this love today to those I meet.

"Then shall the maidens rejoice in the dance, and the young men and the old shall be merry. I will turn their mourning into joy, I will comfort them, and give them gladness for sorrow. I will feast the soul of the priests with abundance, and my people shall be satisfied with my goodness, says the Lord."

Jeremiah 31:13, 14

Life is a mixture
    of sunshine and rain
Laughter and teardrops
    pleasure and pain—
Low tides and high tides,
    mountains and plains,
Triumphs, defeats,
    and losses and gains—
But always in all ways
    God's guiding and leading
And He alone knows
    the things we're most needing—
And when He sends sorrow
    or some dreaded affliction,
Be assured that it comes
    with God's kind benediction—
And if we accept it
    as a gift of His love,
We'll be showered with blessings
    from our Father above.

Times and tides of my life fluctuate and change. Help me, God, to enjoy each one.

Know therefore that the Lord your God is God, the faithful God who keeps covenant and steadfast love with those who love him and keep his command-ments, to a thousand generations.

Deuteronomy 7:9

Dear God. . .
There are things we cannot measure,
Like the depths of waves and sea
And the heights of stars in heaven
And the joy You bring to me,
Like eternity's long endlessness
And the sunset's golden hue,
There is no way to measure
The love I have for You.

My life, my love I offer to You. May I live my life in love for You, in You, and with You, Lord.

The Spirit himself gives witness with our spirit that we are children of God. But if we are children, we are heirs as well: heirs of God, heirs with Christ, if only we suffer with him so as to be glorified with him.

Romans 8:16, 17 NAB

We are all
God's children
and He loves us
every one—
He freely
and completely
forgives all
that we have done,
Asking only
if we're ready
to follow where He leads,
Content that
in His wisdom
He will answer
all our needs.

Father, a good memory is a great gift and talent but the ability to forgive others is a sign of true greatness and to forget the hurts that were inflicted is a richer talent.

Beloved, if God so loved us, we also ought to love one another. No man has ever seen God; if we love one another, God abides in us and his love is perfected in us.

1 John 4:11, 12

God of love—Forgive! Forgive!
Teach us how to truly live,
Ask us not our race or creed,
Just take us in our hour of need,
And let us know You love us, too,
And that we are a part of You. . .
And someday may man realize
That all the earth, the seas, and skies
Belong to God, who made us all,
The rich, the poor, the great, the small,
And in the Father's Holy sight
No man is yellow, black, or white,
And peace on earth cannot be found
Until we meet on common ground
And every man becomes a brother
Who worships God and loves all others.

Gracious God, develop within me an acute awareness of my dependency on You. May I appreciate and attest to Your love for every man, woman, and child. You and I working together can make a difference in someone's life.

"Do not lay up for yourselves treasures on earth, where moth and rust consume and where thieves break in and steal, but lay up for yourselves treasures in heaven, where neither moth nor rust consumes and where thieves do not break in and steal. For where your treasure is, there will your heart be also."

Matthew 6:19–21

Not all of us can triumph
or rise to heights of fame,
And many times what should be ours,
goes to another name—
But he who makes a sacrifice,
so another may succeed,
is indeed a true disciple
of our blessed Savior's creed—
For when we give ourselves away
in sacrifice and love,
We are laying up rich treasures
in God's Kingdom up above—
For any sacrifice on earth,
made in the dear Lord's name,
Assures the giver of a place
in Heaven's Hall of Fame—
And who can say with certainty
Where the greatest talent lies,
Or who will be the greatest
In our Heavenly Father's eyes!

It is ever-amazing, Lord, what can be accomplished if we are not concerned about who gets the credit and praise.

Above all hold unfailing your love for one another, since love covers a multitude of sins.

1 Peter 4:8

Love is a journey through the years
With peaks of joy and vales of tears—
A journey two folks take together
Hand-in-hand through wind and weather. . .
For with the trials of life love grows
Like flowers grow 'neath winter's snows,
And love that once was yours alone
God now has made part of His own. . .
And as you start another year
May you feel His presence near,
And may happiness that's heaven-sent
Fill both of your hearts with joy and content.

My loving and generous God, I sense Your love all around me and specifically, in the one person You sent for me to love and to share my life. May we strive to enjoy the journey together.

Peace & Joy

"I am the door; if any one enters by me, he will be saved, and will go in and out and find pasture."

John 10:9

The better you know God, the better you feel,
For to learn more about Him and discover He's real
Can wholly, completely, and miraculously change,
Reshape and remake and then rearrange
Your mixed-up, miserable, and unhappy life
Adrift on the sea of sin-sickened strife—
But when you once know this Man of good will,
He will calm your life and say, "Peace, be still". . .
So open your heart's door and let Christ come in
And He'll give you new life and free you from sin—
And there is no joy that can ever compare
With the joy of knowing you're in God's care.

Jesus, You are the door which leads to peace and calm. Let me never close You out of my life. May I always stay open to You and to Your message.

A glad heart makes a cheerful countenance, but by sorrow of heart the spirit is broken.

Proverbs 15:13

Cheerful thoughts like sunbeams
Lighten up the darkest fears
For when the heart is happy
There's just no time for tears—
And when the face is smiling
It's impossible to frown
And when you are high-spirited
You cannot feel low-down—
And since fear and dread and worry
Cannot help in any way,
It's much healthier and happier
To be cheerful every day
For when the heart is cheerful
It cannot be filled with fear.
And without fear, the way ahead
Seems more distinct and clear—
And we realize there's nothing
We need ever face alone
For our Heavenly Father loves us
And our problems are His own.

I try to be cheerful, God, but there are so many problems surrounding me. Problems that I alone must solve . . . or do I need to do it alone? Of course not, I have You and with that thought the day seems brighter already.

"You are my lamp, O LORD!
  O my God, you brighten the darkness about me."
                                          2 Samuel 22:29 NAB

For it's not the big celebrity in a world of fame and praise,
But it's doing unpretentiously in undistinguished ways
The work that God assigned to us, unimportant as it
    seems,
That makes our task outstanding and brings reality to
    dreams—
So do not sit and idly wish for wider, new dimensions
Where you can put in practice your many good inten-
    tions
But at the spot God placed you begin at once to do
Little things to brighten up the lives surrounding you,
For if everybody brightened up the spot on which
    they're standing
By being more considerate and a little less demanding,
This dark old world would very soon eclipse the evening
    star
If everybody brightened up the corner where they are!

*Dear Light of the World, help me to "brighten the corner"
wherever I may be. Remind me from time to time, Father, that
the important biographical data is not what I own or where I
live but rather what I am. Let me be someone who follows
through on acts of kindness. One good deed actually accomplished is far more valuable than one hundred intentions left
undone.*

. . . Weeping may tarry for the night, but joy comes with the morning.

Psalms 30:5

There are always two sides,
    the good and the bad,
The dark and the light,
    the sad and the glad—
But in looking back over
    the good and the bad
We're aware of the number
    of good things we've had—
So thank God for good things
    He has already done,
And be grateful to Him
    for the battles you've won,
And know that the same God
    who helped you before
Is ready and willing
    to help you once more—
For always remember
    that whatever betide you,
You are never alone
    for God is beside you.

Jesus, give me a firm resolution to have a positive attitude toward life and its challenges. When problems face me, the problems are not problems unless my attitude toward them make them so.

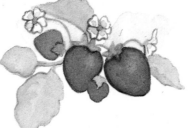

The heart of a man changes his countenance,
either for good or for evil.
The sign of a good heart is a cheerful countenance;
withdrawn and perplexed is the laborious schemer.

Sirach 13:24, 25 NAB

Since fear and dread and worry
Cannot help in any way,
It's much healthier and happier
To be cheerful every day—
And if we'll only try it
We will find, without a doubt,
A cheerful attitude's something
No one should be without—
For when the heart is cheerful
It cannot be filled with fear,
And without fear the way ahead
Seems more distinct and clear—
And we realize there's nothing
We need ever face alone,
For our Heavenly Father loves us
And our problems are His own.

*Father, assist me in my attempts to be cheerful with
whatever problems are facing me. Surely cheer will elimi-
nate my fear.*

O give thanks to the Lord, call on his name, make known his deeds among the peoples! Sing to him, sing praises to him, tell of all his wonderful works! Glory in his holy name; let the hearts of those who seek the Lord rejoice! Seek the Lord and his strength, seek his presence continually!

Psalms 105:1–4

"O, God, our help in ages past,
Our hope in years to be"—
Look down upon this present
And see our need of Thee. . .
For in this age of unrest,
With danger all around,
We need Thy hand to lead us
To higher, safer ground. . .
We need Thy help and counsel
To make us more aware
That our safety and security
Lie solely in Thy care. . .
Give us strength and courage
To be honorable and true
Practicing Your precepts
In everything we do,
And keep us gently humble
In the greatness of Thy Love
So someday we are fit to dwell
With Thee in peace above.

Lord, I know that I matter to You. Please let me live my life so that You know that You matter to me.

And he awoke and rebuked the wind, and said to the sea, "Peace! Be still!" And the wind ceased, and there was a great calm. He said to them, "Why are you afraid? Have you no faith?"

Mark 4:39, 40

Whenever I am troubled
    and lost in deep despair
I bundle all my troubles up
    and go to God in prayer. . .
I tell Him I am heartsick
    and lost and lonely, too,
That my heart is deeply burdened
    and I don't know what to do. . .
But I know He stilled the tempest
    and calmed the angry sea
And I humbly ask if in His love
    He'll do the same for me. . .
And then I just keep quiet
    and think only thoughts of peace
And if I abide in stillness
    my restless murmurings cease.

Jesus, still this tempest within me and calm my uneasy and grumbled complaints. Give me quiet and peace of mind.

"Peace I leave with you; my peace I give to you; not as the world gives do I give to you. Let not your hearts be troubled, neither let them be afraid."

John 14:27

Peace is not something you fight for
With bombs and missiles
that kill,
Peace is attained in the silence
That comes when the heart stands still. . .

For hearts that are restless and warlike
With longings that never cease,
Can never contribute ideas
That bring the world nearer
to peace. . .
For as dew never falls on a morning
That follows a dark stormy night,
The peace and the grace of our Father
Fall not on a soul that's in flight. . .

So if we seek peace for all people
There is but one place
to begin,
And the armament race will not win it
For the fortress of peace
is within.

God of heaven and earth, I beseech You to create a longing for peace within the hearts of each one of us. If peace is to come, it must originate in each person's heart and in each home.

This God—his way is perfect; the promise of the Lord proves true; he is a shield for all those who take refuge in him.

Psalms 18:30

To be in God's keeping
    is surely a blessing,
For though life is often
    dark and distressing,
No day is too dark
    and no burden too great
That God in His love
    cannot penetrate,
And to know and believe
    without question or doubt
That no matter what happens
    God is there to help out,
Is to hold in your hand
    The golden key
To peace and to joy
    and serenity!

Unlock my heart and satisfy these deep longings. Jesus, You are the door to peace for which I am searching. Do not permit me to ever shut You out of my life, rather keep me secure in the knowledge that You are beside me.

Faith & Hope

O Lord, thou art our Father; we are the clay, and thou art our potter; we are all the work of thy hand.

Isaiah 64:8

The future is yours, it belongs to you,
And with faith in God
and in yourself, too,
No hill's too high,
no mountain's too tall,
For with faith in the Lord
you can conquer them all—
And all that you wish for
that is honest and true
The Lord will certainly give to you,
Not always the way you most desire
But always He gives
what you most require—
So accept what He sends,
be it bitter or sweet,
For God knows best
what makes life complete,
And great is your gladness
and rich your reward
When you learn to accept
the will of the Lord.

Master Potter, I am an unfinished work of art with unrealized potential. Please continue to shape and mold this piece of clay as You see fit.

And he said to the woman, "Your faith has saved you, go in peace."

Luke 7:50

When everything is pleasant and bright
And the things we do turn out just right,
We feel without question that God is real,
For, when we are happy, how good we feel. . .
But when the tides turn and gone is the song
And misfortune comes and our plans go wrong,
Doubt creeps in and we start to wonder
And our thoughts about God are torn asunder—
For we feel deserted in time of deep stress,
Without God's presence to assure us and bless. . .
And it is then when our senses are reeling
We realize clearly it's faith and not feeling—
For it takes great faith to patiently wait,
Believing God comes not too soon or too late.

Do what You will with this earthen vessel, Lord. It belongs to You. Pour out the doubts and fill me with faith.

Know that the Lord is God! It is he that made us, and we are his, we are his people, and the sheep of his pasture.

Psalms 100:3

Take the Savior's loving hand
    and do not try to understand,
Just let Him lead you where He will
    through pastures green, by waters still,
And place yourself in His loving care
    and He will gladly help you bear
Whatever lies ahead of you
    He will see you safely through,
No earthly pain is ever too much
    if God bestows His merciful touch.

Lead me where You will, Lord, but please keep hold of my hand.

"Do not let your hearts be troubled. Have faith in
God and faith in me."

John 14:1 NAB

Whatever betide you,
     God is always beside you—
So let not your heart be troubled
     nor your mind be filled with fear
For you have God's reassurance
     that He's always very near,
And no prayer goes unanswered
     and no one walks alone
And if we trust the Savior
     we are never on our own—

*I shall trust in You, the Master Weaver. You are in charge
of my tapestry of life. You have already selected the threads
and the colors. Help me with the pattern.*

. . . When we cry "Abba! Father!" it is the Spirit himself bearing witness with our spirit that we are children of God, and if children, then heirs, heirs of God and fellow heirs with Christ, provided we suffer with him in order that we may also be glorified with him. I consider that the sufferings of this present time are not worth comparing with the glory that is to be revealed to us.

Romans 8:15–18

Our Father knows what's best for us,
So why should we complain—
We always want the sunshine,
But He knows there must be rain—
We love the sound of laughter
And the merriment of cheer,
But our hearts would lose their tenderness
If we never shed a tear. . .
Our Father tests us often
With suffering and with sorrow,
He tests us, not to punish us,
But to help us meet tomorrow. . .
For growing trees are strengthened
When they withstand the storm,
And the sharp cut of the chisel
Gives the marble grace and form. . .
So whenever we are troubled
And when everything goes wrong,
It is just God working in us
To make our spirit strong.

Heavenly Teacher, call me by name and when You put me to the test, I pray that I pass it with acceptable excellence. I know You are preparing me for the future.

Ever since the creation of the world his invisible nature, namely, his eternal power and deity, has been clearly perceived in the things that have been made. . . .

Romans 1:20

Sometimes when faith is running low
And I cannot fathom why things are so. . .
I walk alone among the flowers I grow
And learn the answers to all I would know.
For among my flowers I have come to see
Life's miracle and its mystery. . .
And standing in silence and reverie
My faith comes flooding back to me!

Heavenly Father, give me vision to see the wise and inspirational message that You have placed within a flower. The life of a flower, like the life of a man, is measured not by what others are doing for it, but rather the enjoyment it is giving to others.

A righteous man who walks in his integrity—blessed
are his sons after him!

Proverbs 20:7

> Remember that ideals
>   are like stars up in the sky,
> You can never really reach them,
>   hanging in the heavens high. . .
> But like the mighty mariner
>   who sailed the storm-tossed sea,
> And used the stars to chart his course
>   with skill and certainty,
> You too can chart your course in life
>   with high ideals and love,
> For high ideals are like the stars
>   that light the sky above. . .
> You cannot ever reach them,
>   but lift your heart up high
> And your life will be as shining
>   as the stars up in the sky.

*Speak to me Holy Spirit and make me aware of what is right
and what is wrong in all phases of my life. Help me to resist
the "but everybody is doing it" philosophy.*

Search me, O God, and know my heart! Try me and know my thoughts! And see if there be any wicked way in me, and lead me in the way everlasting!

Psalms 139:23, 24

God, here I am in a chaotic state
Seeking some way to do something great. . .
I want to be someone who contributes to make
A less violent world for everyone's sake. . .
But who can I go to and who can I trust,
Who'll show me the difference between love and
    lust?
I'm willing to listen, I'm willing to do
Whatever it takes to make this world new. . .
But in the confusion and the noise all around
Where can the answer to my question be found?
Dear God up in heaven, hear a fervent plea—
Show me somewhere what You want me to be!

Father, what is the mission or task that You have in mind for me to do? Whatever it may be, show me how and when Your assignment must be done and then help me to accomplish it.

Teach me to do thy will, for thou art my God! . . .
Psalms 143:10

The future
is not ours to know
and it may never be,
So let us live
and give our best
and give it lavishly,
And let us be
content to solve
our problems
one by one,
Asking nothing
of tomorrow except
"Thy will be done."

Dear God, what I am is Your gift to me, what I make of myself is my gift to You. I pray that my gift to You is acceptable and worthwhile.

There are three things that remain—faith, hope, and love—and the greatest of these is love.

1 Corinthians 13:13 TLB

There are three treasures
More priceless than gold.
For if you possess them
You've riches untold—
For with faith to believe
What your eyes cannot see,
And hope to look forward
To joy yet to be.
And love to transform
The most commonplace
Into beauty and kindness
And goodness and grace.
There's nothing too much
To accomplish or do,
For with faith, hope, and love
To carry you through,
Your life will be happy
And full and complete,
For with faith, hope, and love
The bitter turns sweet.

Father, increase my faith, strengthen my hope, and deepen my love so that I can share these treasures.

After that, Jesus, realizing that everything was now finished, said to fulfill the Scripture, "I am thirsty."

John 19:28 NAB

A troubled world can find
Blessed reassurance
And enduring peace of mind
For though we grow discouraged
In this world we're living in,
There is comfort just in knowing
God has triumphed over sin
For our Savior's Resurrection
Was God's way of telling men
That in Christ we are eternal
And in Him we live again.

Thank You, God, for sending Your Son to redeem us and thank You, Jesus, for sacrificing Your life for us. The reassurance of life after death is the greatest of comforts.

If you found any beauty in the poems of this book
Or some peace and comfort in a word or line
Don't give me praise or wordly acclaim
For the words that you read are not mine . . .
I borrowed them all to share with you
From our Heavenly Father above,
And the joy that you felt was God speaking to you
As He flooded your heart with His Love.

H.S.R.

And if you receive hope or strength
From the Scripture or from the prayer
Know that whenever or wherever you read this,
our Heavenly Father is there!

V.J.R.